EASY INSTRUMENTAL DUETS   CELLOS

BROADWAY SONGS
FOR TWO

Arrangements by Peter Deneff

ISBN 978-1-5400-1289-0

7777 W. BLUEMOUND RD. P.O. BOX 13819 MILWAUKEE, WI 53213

Visit Hal Leonard Online at
www.halleonard.com

CONTENTS

ANY DREAM WILL DO

from JOSEPH AND THE AMAZING TECHNICOLOR® DREAMCOAT

CELLOS

Music by ANDREW LLOYD WEBBER
Lyrics by TIM RICE

BRING HIM HOME

from LES MISÉRABLES

Music by CLAUDE-MICHEL SCHÖNBERG
Lyrics by HERBERT KRETZMER
and ALAIN BOUBLIL

CELLOS

CABARET
from the Musical CABARET

CELLOS

Words by FRED EBB
Music by JOHN KANDER

EDELWEISS
from THE SOUND OF MUSIC

CELLOS

Lyrics by OSCAR HAMMERSTEIN II
Music by RICHARD RODGERS

FOR FOREVER

from DEAR EVAN HANSEN

CELLOS

Music and Lyrics by BENJ PASEK
and JUSTIN PAUL

HELLO, DOLLY!

from HELLO, DOLLY!

CELLOS

Music and Lyric by
JERRY HERMAN

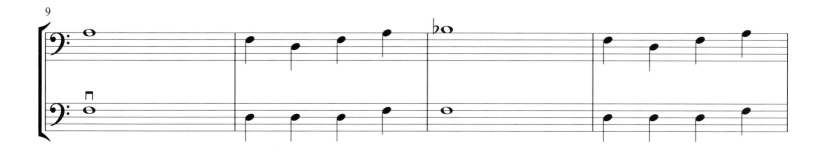

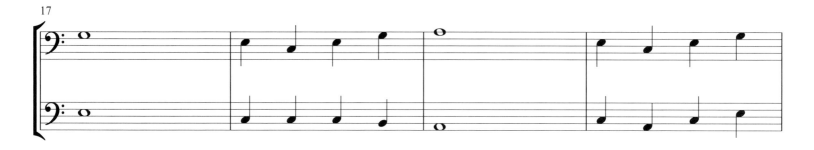

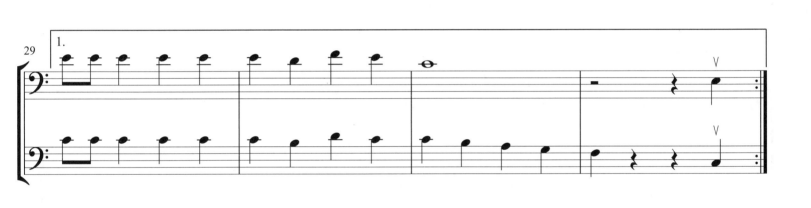

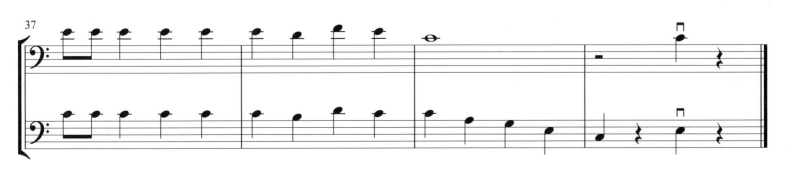

I BELIEVE

from the Broadway Musical THE BOOK OF MORMON

CELLOS

Words and Music by TREY PARKER,
ROBERT LOPEZ and MATT STONE

I WHISTLE A HAPPY TUNE

from THE KING AND I

CELLOS

Lyrics by OSCAR HAMMERSTEIN II
Music by RICHARD RODGERS

IF I WERE A BELL
from GUYS AND DOLLS

CELLOS

By FRANK LOESSER

THE IMPOSSIBLE DREAM
(The Quest)
from MAN OF LA MANCHA

CELLOS

Lyric by JOE DARION
Music by MITCH LEIGH

MAMMA MIA
from MAMMA MIA!

CELLOS

Words and Music by BENNY ANDERSSON,
BJÖRN ULVAEUS and STIG ANDERSON

MEMORY
from CATS

CELLOS

Music by ANDREW LLOYD WEBBER
Text by TREVOR NUNN after T.S. ELIOT

MY FAVORITE THINGS
from THE SOUND OF MUSIC

CELLOS

Lyrics by OSCAR HAMMERSTEIN II
Music by RICHARD RODGERS

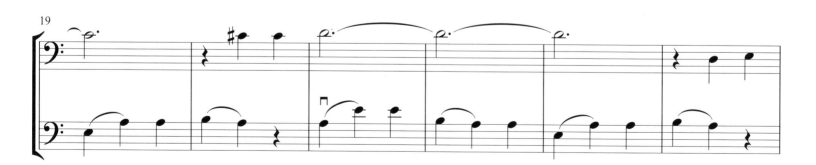

ONE
from A CHORUS LINE

CELLOS

Music by MARVIN HAMLISCH
Lyric by EDWARD KLEBAN

POPULAR
from the Broadway Musical WICKED

CELLOS

Music and Lyrics by
STEPHEN SCHWARTZ

SEASONS OF LOVE

from RENT

CELLOS

Words and Music by
JONATHAN LARSON

Moderately

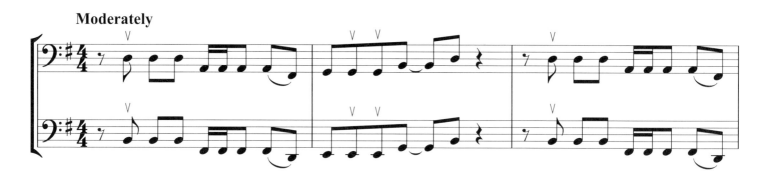

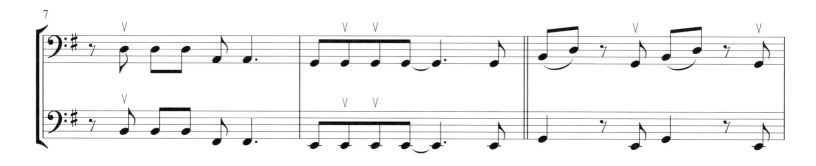

SEVENTY SIX TROMBONES

from Meredith Willson's THE MUSIC MAN

CELLOS

By MEREDITH WILLSON

SUMMERTIME
from PORGY AND BESS®

Cellos

Music and Lyrics by GEORGE GERSHWIN,
DuBOSE and DOROTHY HEYWARD
and IRA GERSHWIN

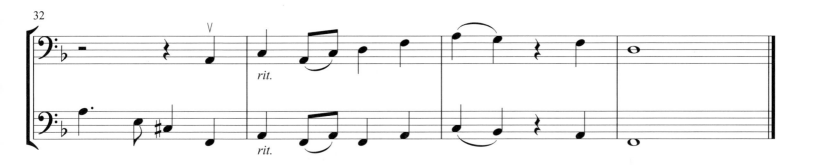

SUNRISE, SUNSET

from the Musical FIDDLER ON THE ROOF

Words by SHELDON HARNICK
Music by JERRY BOCK

CELLOS

TOMORROW

from the Musical Production ANNIE

CELLOS

Lyric by MARTIN CHARNIN
Music by CHARLES STROUSE

WHERE IS LOVE?
from the Broadway Musical OLIVER!

CELLOS

Words and Music by
LIONEL BART

YOU'VE GOT A FRIEND

featured in BEAUTIFUL: THE CAROLE KING MUSICAL

CELLOS

Words and Music by
CAROLE KING

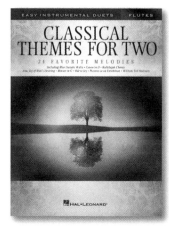

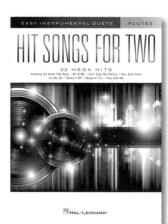